Better Homes and Ga...

SNACK ATTACK
RETURN OF THE MUNCHIES

COOKIES

Meredith® Books,
Des Moines, Iowa

Better Homes and Gardens® Snack Attack: Return of the Munchies
Editor: Sheena Chihak
Contributing Graphic Designer: Mada Design, Inc.
Copy Chief: Doug Kouma
Copy Editor: Kevin Cox
Publishing Operations Manager: Karen Schirm
Edit and Design Production Coordinator: Mary Lee Gavin
Editorial Assistant: Sheri Cord
Book Production Managers: Marjorie J. Schenkelberg,
    Mark Weaver
Contributing Photographer: Adam Albright, William Hopkins
Contributing Illustrator: Dave Titus Illustrations
Contributing Copy Editor: Joy English
Contributing Proofreaders: Karen Grossman, Lynn Stratton,
    Staci Scheurenbrand
Contributing Indexer: Elizabeth Parson
Test Kitchen Director: Lynn Blanchard
Test Kitchen Product Supervisor: Colleen Weeden
Test Kitchen Culinary Specialists: Marilyn Cornelius, Juliana Hale,
    Maryellyn Krantz, Jill Moberly, Colleen Weeden, Lori Wilson
Test Kitchen Nutrition Specialists: Elizabeth Burt, R.D.,L.D.;
    Laura Marzen, R.D., L.D.

Meredith® Books
Editorial Director: John Riha
Managing Editor: Kathleen Armentrout
Deputy Editor: Jennifer Darling
Brand Manager: Janell Pittman
Group Editor: Jan Miller
Senior Associate Design Director: Mick Schnepf

Director, Marketing and Publicity: Amy Nichols
Executive Director, Sales: Ken Zagor
Director, Operations: George A. Susral
Director, Production: Douglas M. Johnston
Business Director: Janice Croat

Vice President and General Manager, SIM: Jeff Myers

Better Homes and Gardens® **Magazine**
Editor in Chief: Gayle Goodson Butler
Deputy Editor, Food and Entertaining: Nancy Hopkins

Meredith Publishing Group
President: Jack Griffin
Executive Vice President: Doug Olson

Meredith Corporation
Chairman of the Board: William T. Kerr
President and Chief Executive Officer: Stephen M. Lacy

In Memoriam: E. T. Meredith III (1933–2003)

Test Kitchen

Our seal assures you that every recipe in *Snack Attack: Return of the Munchies* has been tested in the Better Homes and Gardens® Test Kitchen. This means that each recipe is practical and reliable, and meets our high standards of taste appeal. We guarantee your satisfaction with this book for as long as you own it.

CONTENTS

SNACK TIME

When hunger strikes and your next meal is hours away, check this out: *Snack Attack: Return of the Munchies*, a cookbook loaded with awesome munchies just for you! These super snacks will refuel you for a busy afternoon jam-packed with activities.

Chomp on ChocoNutty Sandwiches, Nuts-About-Fruit Salad, and Rocky Road Popcorn, or get ready for the big game with Home Run Chicken Salad or Hang Ten Cinnamon Scoops. Then lace up your hiking boots and get ready for the ultimate snacking adventure on a world tour! You'll stop in Mexico for quesadillas, in China for wontons, and in a tropical paradise for delicious fruit salad. You'll find the perfect snack for any situation. So what are you waiting for? The adventure starts in the kitchen! Pick a recipe, grab your ingredients, and follow the directions. In no time you'll be chowing down on tasty treats that will stop hunger in its tracks!

FOOD RULES!

Before you start mixing and mashing, there are some kitchen basics and food safety rules you need to know.

On Your Mark:

- Read the entire recipe from beginning to end. Ask yourself: Do I know exactly what I'm supposed to do? If there's anything you don't understand, ask an adult for help.

- Check your ingredients. Make sure you have enough of all the required ingredients. If you don't, make a list of what you need and ask an adult to help you get them.

- Check your utensils. Gather all the equipment you'll need to complete the recipe. If you're missing anything, ask an adult for help.

Get Set:

- Wash fresh fruits and veggies in cool water before eating or preparing them.

- Never use cracked or dirty eggs. After working with eggs, wash your hands, equipment, and countertop.

- Always wash your hands with soap and water for at least 20 seconds before you start cooking.

Go!

- Measure ingredients accurately.

- It's usually best to finish each step in the recipe before starting the next.

- Use good food-safety habits.

Victory Lap:

- Put leftovers away as soon as possible.

- Put away all ingredients and equipment. Load dirty dishes in the dishwasher or wash and dry them. Wipe counters with hot, soapy water. Wipe the table clean.

- Throw away trash such as food wrappers and empty packages.

SUNNY DAY PARFAITS

Brighten anyone's day with these sweet treats and have a taste of summer vacation whenever you want!

UTENSILS

Measuring spoons
Small mixing bowl
Rubber scraper
Measuring cups
2 parfait glasses

INGREDIENTS

1   8-ounce carton low-fat piña colada yogurt or other low-fat yogurt
¼   teaspoon vanilla
¼   cup frozen light whipped dessert topping, thawed
1   cup cubed mango or papaya
½   cup sliced fresh strawberries
1   tablespoon toasted shredded coconut, if you like
    Graham cracker sticks, if you like

HOW TO MAKE IT

1   Put yogurt and vanilla in the bowl. Use the rubber scraper to combine. Gently stir in whipped topping.

2   Put ½ cup of the mango or papaya in each parfait glass. Top each with a fourth of the yogurt mixture. Top each with ¼ cup of the strawberries and half of the remaining yogurt mixture. If you like, sprinkle each with coconut and garnish with graham cracker sticks. Serve the parfaits immediately.

    Makes 2 servings

NUTRITION FACTS PER SERVING:
219 calories, 4 g total fat, 5 mg cholesterol, 79 mg sodium, 42 g carbohydrate, 3 g fiber, 6 g protein

TAKE A DIP

UTENSILS

Cutting board
Sharp knife
Small mixing bowl
Electric mixer
Rubber scraper
Measuring cups
Measuring spoons

INGREDIENTS

½ 8-ounce package reduced-fat cream cheese (Neufchâtel)

½ cup creamy peanut butter

2 to 3 tablespoons milk

2 teaspoons honey

Celery sticks, animal crackers, and/or assorted dippers such as peeled jicama sticks, carrot sticks, apple wedges, pear wedges, or graham cracker sticks

PEANUT BUTTER DIP

HOW TO MAKE IT

1 Place the cream cheese in the small bowl. Let cream cheese stand at room temperature in the bowl for 30 minutes to soften.

2 Beat cream cheese with the electric mixer on medium speed until smooth. Turn off the mixer and scrape the sides of the bowl with the rubber scraper. Add peanut butter, milk, and honey. Beat with the electric mixer on medium speed until smooth. Turn off the mixer.

3 Serve the dip with assorted dippers. (Cover and chill any remaining peanut butter dip up to 24 hours.)

Makes about 1¼ cups

NUTRITION FACTS PER SERVING:
(per 1 tablespoon dip with dippers)
56 calories, 5 g total fat, 4 mg cholesterol, 53 mg sodium, 2 g carbohydrate, 0 g fiber, 2 g protein

UTENSILS

Measuring cups

Blender or food processor

Measuring spoons

Rubber scraper

Serving bowl

Airtight storage container
   (if chilling)

INGREDIENTS

1   cup peeled sliced peaches, sliced strawberries, mandarin orange sections, and/or cubed fresh pineapple

1   8-ounce carton light dairy sour cream

1   8-ounce package reduced-fat cream cheese (Neufchâtel)

½   teaspoon finely shredded orange peel

1   teaspoon vanilla

   Fat-free milk, if needed

CREAMY FRUIT DIP

HOW TO MAKE IT

1   Place the fruit in the blender or food processor. Cover the blender or food processor with lid and blend or process until smooth. Turn off the blender or food processor. Add sour cream, cream cheese, orange peel, and vanilla. Cover the blender or food processor with lid and blend or process until smooth.

2   Pour mixture into the serving bowl using the rubber scraper to get all the dip out of the blender or food processor. Serve the dip immediately or place in the airtight container and chill up to 24 hours. If the dip is too thick after chilling, stir in fat-free milk, 1 tablespoon at a time, to reach desired consistency.

Makes about 2⅓ cups

NUTRITION FACTS PER SERVING:

(per 1 tablespoon dip with dippers)
26 calories, 2 g total fat, 7 mg cholesterol, 28 mg sodium, 1 g carbohydrate, 0 g fiber, 1 g protein

With plenty to share, these dips are sure to make a big splash with your friends.

COWBOY CAL'S BEANS AND SALSA

This Wild West dip will have everyone rounded up for some grub faster than you can say, "Ride 'em, cowboy!"

NUTRITION FACTS PER SERVING:
205 calories, 10 g total fat, 23 mg cholesterol, 579 mg sodium,
21 g carbohydrate, 4 g fiber, 9 g protein

UTENSILS

Can opener
Measuring cups
Medium saucepan
Wooden spoon
Hot pads
9-inch pie plate or shallow dish
Small mixing bowl
Wire whisk
Small spoon

INGREDIENTS

1   16-ounce can refried beans
1   cup mild salsa
1   cup shredded cheddar cheese
    Shredded cheddar cheese,
    salsa, shredded lettuce,
    if you like
    Sour cream, if you like
    Tortilla chips

HOW TO MAKE IT

1   Put the beans, 1 cup salsa, and 1 cup shredded cheese in the saucepan. Use the wooden spoon to combine. Put the saucepan on the burner. Turn the burner to medium heat. Cook until the cheese melts. Stir occasionally with the wooden spoon. Turn off the burner. Use the hot pads to remove the pan from the burner.

2   Spoon the bean mixture into the 9-inch pie plate or shallow dish. Top with additional shredded cheese, salsa, and lettuce, if you like. Serve with tortilla chips and, if you like, sour cream.

Makes 8 servings

SMOOTHIE SAILING

BANANA-BERRY SMOOTHIES

UTENSILS

Cutting board
Table knife
Measuring cups
Electric blender
3 serving glasses
Rubber scraper

INGREDIENTS

2 small ripe bananas

1 cup frozen unsweetened whole strawberries

1 8-ounce carton vanilla low-fat yogurt

3/4 cup fat-free milk

Fresh whole strawberries, if you like

HOW TO MAKE IT

1 Remove the peel from the bananas and throw away. Place the bananas on the cutting board. Use the knife to cut bananas into chunks.

2 Put banana chunks, frozen strawberries, yogurt, and milk in the blender.

3 Cover the blender with the lid and blend on high speed until the mixture is smooth. Turn off the blender. Pour mixture into the serving glasses. Use the rubber scraper to get all of the drink out of the blender. If you like, top the drinks with whole strawberries.
Makes 3 servings

After some serious studying you need a snack that's a breeze. Choosing a flavor is the hardest part of these easy freezies.

NUTRITION FACTS PER SERVING:
182 calories, 3 g total fat, 9 mg cholesterol, 82 mg sodium, 35 g carbohydrate, 3 g fiber, 7 g protein

UTENSILS

Cutting board
Table knife
Measuring cups
Measuring spoons, if you like
Electric blender
Rubber scraper
6 serving glasses

INGREDIENTS

2 small ripe bananas

2/3 cup refrigerated mango slices, drained

1 12-ounce can mango, peach, apricot, or other fruit nectar, chilled

1 cup plain fat-free yogurt

1 tablespoon honey, if you like

Cut-up fresh fruit such as bananas, peeled kiwifruit, and/or peeled mango, if you like

TANGO-MANGO SMOOTHIES

HOW TO MAKE IT

1 Remove the peel from the bananas and throw away. Place the bananas on the cutting board. Use the knife to cut bananas into chunks.

2 Put banana chunks, mango slices, fruit nectar, yogurt, and, if you like, honey in the blender.

3 Cover the blender with lid and blend on high speed until smooth. Turn off the blender. Pour mixture into the serving glasses. Use the rubber scraper to get all of the drink out of the blender. If you like, top the drinks with cut-up fresh fruit.

Makes 6 servings

NUTRITION FACTS PER SERVING:
108 calories, 0 g total fat,1 mg cholesterol, 33 mg sodium,
24 g carbohydrate, 1 g fiber, 3 g protein

CRUNCHY FRUIT SUNDAES

Your parents will be bowled over when they see you snacking on this crunchy creation.

NUTRITION FACTS PER SERVING:
146 calories, 2 g total fat, 7 mg cholesterol,
150 mg sodium, 24 g carbohydrate,
2 g fiber, 7 g protein

UTENSILS

Cutting board
Sharp knife
Measuring cups
Small spoon
2 serving bowls
Measuring spoons

INGREDIENTS

1 cup assorted fresh fruit such as blueberries, grapes, strawberries, and/or bananas

1 8-ounce carton vanilla low-fat yogurt

½ to 1 cup ready-to-eat cereal, such as round toasted oat cereal

1 tablespoon almonds or walnuts, if you like

HOW TO MAKE IT

1 If you are using the strawberries, place them on the cutting board. Use the knife to cut off the green tops. Throw the green tops away. Cut the strawberries into bite-size pieces. If you are using the bananas, remove the peels and throw away. Place the bananas on the cutting board. Use the knife to cut into bite-size pieces.

2 Divide the yogurt in half and spoon each half into a serving bowl. Divide cereal and fruit in half and place into bowls with yogurt. If you like, top with almonds or walnuts. Serve sundaes immediately.

Makes 2 servings

MINI COCOA FRUIT TARTS

Customize a cookie with your favorite spread and fruit for a personalized snack like no other.

UTENSILS

Cutting board
Sharp knife
Measuring cups
Table knife
Measuring spoons

INGREDIENTS

1 large banana, 2 kiwifruit, and/or 1 cup berries, such as strawberries, blueberries, or raspberries

4 purchased large (3-inch) chocolate cookies

¼ cup tub-style light cream cheese with strawberries, chocolate-hazelnut spread, or fudge ice cream topping

2 tablespoons shredded coconut

NUTRITION FACTS PER SERVING:
187 calories, 9 g total fat, 23 mg cholesterol,
116 mg sodium, 26 g carbohydrate, 2 g fiber, 2 g protein

HOW TO MAKE IT

1 If you are using the banana, remove the peel and throw away. Place the banana on the cutting board. Use the sharp knife to cut the banana into bite-size pieces. If you are using the kiwi, have an adult remove the peel. Place the kiwi on the cutting board. Use the sharp knife to cut kiwi into bite-size pieces. If you are using the strawberries, place them on the cutting board. Use the sharp knife to cut off the green tops. Throw the green tops away. Cut the strawberries into bite-size pieces.

2 Use the table knife to spread the flat side of each cookie with 1 tablespoon of the cream cheese, chocolate-hazelnut spread, or ice cream topping. Sprinkle with coconut and top with banana, kiwi, and/or strawberries. Serve the tarts immediately.

Makes 4 tarts

GREAT GRAPE DUNKERS

Take your grapes for a peanut butter plunge with this sweet and salty treat that will sink hunger.

NUTRITION FACTS PER SERVING:
267 calories, 12 g total fat, 1 mg cholesterol,
203 mg sodium, 37 g carbohydrate, 1 g fiber, 3 g protein

UTENSILS

Scissors
Serving platter
Measuring cups
Medium mixing bowl
Electric mixer
Rubber scraper
Serving bowl
Measuring spoons

INGREDIENTS

1   1-pound bunch red and/or green seedless grapes

1/3   cup plain low-fat yogurt

2/3   cup creamy peanut butter

1   8-ounce container frozen whipped dessert topping, thawed

1   tablespoon finely chopped peanuts

Ground cinnamon or cinnamon-sugar

HOW TO MAKE IT

1   Use the scissors to cut the grapes into bunches and place on the serving platter.

2   Put yogurt and peanut butter in the bowl. Beat with the electric mixer on medium-high speed until combined. Stop the mixer. Add whipped topping. Beat on medium-high speed until combined. Turn off the mixer. Use the rubber scraper to move the yogurt mixture to the serving bowl. Sprinkle yogurt mixture with peanuts and cinnamon or cinnamon-sugar. Serve yogurt mixture immediately with grapes.

Makes 8 servings

SODA FLOATS

UTENSILS

Measuring cups
1 tall glass
Long table spoon
Ice cream scoop

INGREDIENTS

1/4   cup chocolate syrup
1/2   cup carbonated water
1/3   cup vanilla ice cream

CHOCOLATE SODA

HOW TO MAKE IT

1   Pour chocolate syrup into the glass.
    Pour carbonated water into the glass;
    stir well with the spoon. Top with ice
    cream. Serve soda immediately.

    Makes 1 serving

NUTRITION FACTS PER SERVING:
288 calories, 5 g total fat, 19 mg cholesterol, 110 mg sodium,
60 g carbohydrate, 1 g fiber, 3 g protein

UTENSILS

Ice cream scoop

1 or 2 tall soda glasses

Measuring cups

Measuring spoons

INGREDIENTS

2 to 3	scoops vanilla ice cream
½ to ¾	cup carbonated water, chilled
3	tablespoons fruit punch concentrate, thawed

FRUITY CREAM SODA

HOW TO MAKE IT

1 Put ice cream in the soda glass. Fill the glass with carbonated water. Drizzle thawed fruit punch concentrate over ice cream. Serve soda immediately.

Makes 1 to 2 servings

Make a sweet ending to your afternoon with these fun, foamy drinks that are perfect for slurping.

NUTRITION FACTS PER SERVING:
237 calories, 8 g total fat, 32 mg cholesterol, 88 mg sodium, 40 g carbohydrate, 1 g fiber, 3 g protein

![GAME DAY]

PERFECT TEN TOSTADAS

Earn a perfect score when you serve this tostada piled high with meat, veggies, and cheese. It's a snack to flip for!

NUTRITION FACTS PER SERVING:
174 calories, 8 g total fat, 40 mg cholesterol, 645 mg sodium, 14 g carbohydrate, 2 g fiber, 9 g protein

UTENSILS

Measuring cups

Small saucepan

Wooden spoon

Hot pads

Serving platter

INGREDIENTS

1½ cups taco sauce with
shredded chicken
(½ of an 18-ounce tub)

4   6-inch tostada shells

¾   cup shredded carrot,
packaged shredded broccoli
(broccoli slaw mix), and/or
canned black beans, rinsed
and drained

⅓   cup shredded Colby and
Monterey Jack cheese

HOW TO MAKE IT

1   Put the chicken mixture in the saucepan. Place the
pan on the burner. Turn the burner to medium heat.
Cook until the chicken is heated through, stirring now
and then with the wooden spoon. Turn off the burner.
Use the hot pads to remove the pan from the burner.

2   Place the tostada shells on the serving platter. Use
the wooden spoon to divide the heated chicken
mixture evenly among the tostada shells. Sprinkle
each tostada with carrot, broccoli, and/or beans.
Sprinkle each tostada with cheese.

Makes 4 servings

27

HOME RUN CHICKEN SALAD

NUTRITION FACTS PER SERVING:
173 calories, 11 g total fat, 54 mg cholesterol, 310 mg sodium,
3 g carbohydrate, 0 g fiber, 16 g protein

UTENSILS

Measuring cups

Measuring spoons

Small mixing bowl

Wooden spoon

Airtight storage container

INGREDIENTS

1/3 cup chopped or shredded cooked chicken or turkey

2 tablespoons chopped celery

1 tablespoon light mayonnaise or salad dressing

1 tablespoon salsa

1 tablespoon shredded cheddar cheese

Shredded lettuce, if you like

Tortilla chips, if you like

HOW TO MAKE IT

1 Put chicken, celery, mayonnaise or salad dressing, salsa, and cheese in the bowl. Use the wooden spoon to combine. Put chicken mixture in the airtight container and chill 1 to 4 hours.

2 If you like, serve the chicken salad on top of the shredded lettuce; or, if you like, use tortilla chips to scoop up the salad.

Makes 1 serving

This classic chicken dish served with your favorite chips will make you a kitchen all-star.

VICTORY VEGGIES

UTENSILS

Wooden spoon

Serving bowl

Measuring cups

Measuring spoons, if you like

INGREDIENTS

1   12-ounce package frozen broccoli and cauliflower in microwaveable steaming bag

1   cup shredded American cheese

2   tablespoons toasted chopped walnuts, if you like

NUTRITION FACTS PER SERVING:
158 calories, 11 g total fat,
27 mg cholesterol, 445 mg sodium,
5 g carbohydrate, 2 g fiber, 8 g protein

LIGHTNING-FAST VEGGIES

HOW TO MAKE IT

1   Steam vegetables in the microwave according to package directions. Use the wooden spoon to transfer vegetables to the serving bowl. Stir in cheese and let stand 1 minute. Stir until cheese is melted and the vegetables are coated. If you like, sprinkle with the walnuts.

Makes 4 servings

RACIN' RICE AND BROCCOLI
HOW TO MAKE IT

1   Put frozen broccoli, uncooked rice, water, and salt in the saucepan. Place the pan on the burner. Turn the burner to medium heat. Bring the mixture to boiling. Stir frequently with the wooden spoon to break up the frozen broccoli. Turn off the burner. Use the hot pads to remove the pan from the burner.

2   Cover the pan and let stand for 5 minutes. Return the pan to the burner. Turn the burner to low heat. Add the cheese to the pan. Stir constantly with the wooden spoon just until cheese is melted. Turn off the burner.

3   Use the wooden spoon to move the rice mixture to a serving bowl. If you like, sprinkle rice mixture with additional cheese.

Makes 6 servings

NUTRITION FACTS PER SERVING:
132 calories, 4 g total fat, 13 mg cholesterol, 270 mg sodium, 16 g carbohydrate, 1 g fiber, 7 g protein

Easy cheesy veggies will get you up to speed when a growling stomach is hot on your heels.

DIVE IN CHEESEBURGER DIP

NUTRITION FACTS PER SERVING:
110 calories, 7g total fat, 26 mg cholesterol, 365mg sodium,
5g carbohydrate, 0g fiber, 8g protein

UTENSILS

Large skillet with lid
Wooden spoon
Hot pads
Colander
Medium mixing bowl
Disposable container for fat
Measuring cups
Measuring spoons
Serving bowl

INGREDIENTS

1   pound lean ground beef
1   15-ounce jar cheese sauce
½   cup ketchup
¼   cup yellow mustard
1   teaspoon purchased
     minced garlic
¼   cup sweet pickle relish,
     if you like
     Scoop-shaped corn chips

For a swimming good time, invite the team over to dive into this yummy dip. Goggles not required.

HOW TO MAKE IT

1   Put ground beef in the skillet. Use the wooden spoon to break up the meat. Place the skillet on the burner. Turn the burner to medium-high heat. Cook until no pink color is left in the meat, stirring now and then with the wooden spoon. This will take 8 to 10 minutes. Turn off the burner. Use the hot pads to remove the skillet from the burner.

2   Place the colander over the bowl. Spoon meat into the colander and let the fat drain into the bowl. Spoon meat back into the skillet. Put the fat into the container to throw away.

3   Add cheese sauce, ketchup, mustard, garlic, and, if you like, pickle relish to the skillet. Cover the skillet with the lid and return skillet to the burner. Turn the burner to medium heat. Cook for 5 minutes. Stir with the wooden spoon after about 3 minutes. Turn off the burner. Use the hot pads to remove the skillet from the burner. Use the wooden spoon to move the meat mixture to the serving bowl. Serve the dip immediately with corn chips.

Makes 16 ¼-cup servings

HANG TEN CINNAMON SCOOPS

Catch the wave with these sweet, crispy scoops and you'll never wipe out.

NUTRITION FACTS PER SERVING:
136 calories, 1 g total fat, 0 mg cholesterol, 60 mg sodium,
30 g carbohydrate, 1 g fiber, 1 g protein

UTENSILS

Cutting board
Sharp knife
Large baking sheet
Measuring spoons
Small mixing bowl
Small spoon
Hot pads
Pancake turner
Wire cooling rack

INGREDIENTS

2   7- to 8-inch flour tortillas
     Nonstick cooking spray
2   teaspoons sugar
¼   teaspoon ground cinnamon
4   4-ounce cups fruit-flavor or
     plain applesauce

HOW TO MAKE IT

1   Turn on the oven to 375°F. Place the tortillas on the cutting board. Use the knife to cut each tortilla into 8 wedges. Place the wedges on the ungreased baking sheet. Generously coat the wedges with cooking spray.

2   Put sugar and cinnamon in the bowl. Stir with the spoon to combine. Sprinkle the sugar mixture over the wedges.

3   Put the baking sheet in the oven. Bake for 7 to 9 minutes or until light brown. Turn off the oven. Use the hot pads to remove the baking sheet from the oven. Use the pancake turner to transfer the wedges to the wire rack. Cool completely. Serve with applesauce.

Makes 4 servings

SLAM DUNK SALADS

For a quick rebound when your energy is running low, try one of these simple salads and you're sure to score big!

HOW TO MAKE IT

BLT Salad:

Put a 10-ounce package of your favorite salad greens into a large bowl. Top with 15 cherry tomatoes, halved, and ½ cup cooked bacon pieces. Sprinkle with 1 cup of your favorite bite-size crackers, if you like. Pour ¾ cup of bottled tomato bacon or ranch dressing over the salad. Toss the ingredients together with two large spoons until combined.

Makes 10 servings

HOW TO MAKE iT

A Bite of Italy Salad:

Cook 8 ounces tricolor pasta according to package directions. Rinse with cold water; drain well. Put the pasta in a large bowl. Add one 2¼-ounce can sliced pitted ripe olives, drained; 15 cherry tomatoes, halved; 1 cup chopped fresh broccoli; 15 slices pepperoni; and 4 ounces cubed cheddar cheese. Pour 1 cup of bottled creamy Italian dressing over the salad. Stir with a wooden spoon until mixed. Cover and chill for 2 hours before serving.

Makes 10 to 12 servings

HOW TO MAKE iT

Fast! Fun! Fruity! Salad

In a large bowl put 1 banana, sliced; 2 handfuls of grapes; 3 peach halves, cut up; 4 strawberries, halved; 5 pineapple chunks; 6 orange sections, halved; and 7 apple slices, halved. In a small bowl stir 8 ounces vanilla yogurt with 1 tablespoon honey, and 2 tablespoons orange juice. Pour yogurt mixture over fruit. Stir with a wooden spoon until combined.

Makes 6 to 8 servings

KICKIN' S'MORES

These gooey treats might dribble a little, but with the combo of chocolate and marshmallow you're sure to score!

NUTRITION FACTS PER SERVING:
63 calories, 1 g total fat, 0 mg cholesterol, 56 mg sodium,
14 g carbohydrate, 0 g fiber, 0 g protein

UTENSILS

Microwave-safe plate

Table knife

Measuring spoons

Measuring cups

Small spoon

INGREDIENTS

4   graham crackers, quartered

4   teaspoons fudge
    ice cream topping

64 miniature marshmallows
    (about ¾ cup)

4   teaspoons strawberry jam

HOW TO MAKE IT

1   Place 8 of the graham cracker quarters on the microwave-safe plate. Use the knife to spread the ice cream topping evenly on the quarters. Place 8 marshmallows on each quarter.

2   Microwave, uncovered, on 100% power (high) for 30 seconds. Spoon the jam evenly over the marshmallows and quickly top with the remaining graham cracker quarters. Serve the s'mores immediately.

Makes 4 servings

Peanut Butter S'mores:

Prepare s'mores as directed, except use chocolate graham cracker squares and substitute peanut butter for ice cream topping. Omit jam.

MATCH POINT MALTS

NUTRITION FACTS PER SERVING:
233 calories, 8 g total fat, 7 mg cholesterol, 150 mg sodium,
40 g carbohydrate, 7 g fiber, 7 g protein

UTENSILS

Ice cream scoop

Measuring cups

Electric blender

Measuring spoons, if needed

Rubber scraper

Serving glasses

INGREDIENTS

1   quart low-fat or light chocolate ice cream, slightly softened

$1/3$ cup fat-free milk

$1/3$ cup chocolate instant malted milk powder

$1/4$ cup creamy peanut butter

Milk, if needed

Coarsely chopped peanuts, if you like

Miniature sandwich cookies, if you like

Miniature marshmallows, if you like

HOW TO MAKE IT

1   Use the ice cream scoop to place half of the ice cream (2 cups) in the blender. Add the $1/3$ cup milk, malted milk powder, and peanut butter to the blender. Cover the blender with the lid. Blend on medium speed until smooth. Turn off the blender. Scoop remaining ice cream (2 cups) into the blender. Cover the blender with the lid. Blend on medium speed until smooth. If necessary, add additional milk, 1 tablespoon at a time, until malts are of desired consistency. Turn off the blender.

2   Use the rubber scraper to pour the malt mixture into the glasses. If you like, top each malt with the chopped peanuts, sandwich cookies, and marshmallows.

Makes 6 servings

When it's time to rally, try these creamy malts and it will be game-set-match to you!

GRAB AND GO

ROCKY ROAD POPCORN

If there are rough roads ahead, take along some candy-coated popcorn to make the trip smooth sailing.

NUTRITION FACTS PER SERVING:
360 calories, 25 g total fat, 0 mg cholesterol, 147 mg sodium, 30 g carbohydrate, 3 g fiber, 8 g protein

UTENSILS

Large baking sheet
Foil
Large saucepan
Measuring spoons
Wooden spoon
Hot pads
Very large mixing bowl
Measuring cups
Airtight storage container

INGREDIENTS

 Nonstick cooking spray
12 ounces chocolate-flavor
 candy coating, chopped
2 tablespoons peanut butter
7 cups plain popped popcorn
2 cups peanuts
1 cup crisp rice cereal
1 cup miniature marshmallows

HOW TO MAKE IT

1 Line the baking sheet with foil and lightly coat with cooking spray. Save until Step 4.

2 Put candy coating and peanut butter in the saucepan. Place the pan on the burner. Turn the burner to low heat. Cook until melted and smooth. Use the wooden spoon to stir frequently. Turn off the burner. Use the hot pads to remove the pan from the burner.

3 While the chocolate is melting, put the popcorn, peanuts, cereal, and marshmallows in the bowl. Use a clean wooden spoon to combine. Pour the warm melted chocolate mixture over the popcorn mixture. Use the wooden spoon to stir well so all of the popcorn mixture is coated.

4 Spread popcorn mixture onto the prepared baking sheet. Let stand at room temperature for 30 minutes or until cool. Break apart into clusters. Store in the airtight container at room temperature up to 2 days.

Makes about 12 cups

FRUIT AND PEANUTTY POCKETS

NUTRITION FACTS PER SERVING:
239 calories, 10 g total fat, 0 mg cholesterol, 240 mg sodium,
31 g carbohydrate, 3 g fiber, 8 g protein

UTENSILS

Table knife

Measuring cups

Measuring spoons

Small spoon

Plastic wrap, if you like

INGREDIENTS

2 large white or whole wheat pita bread rounds, halved crosswise

¼ cup chunky peanut butter

¼ cup raisins

1 cup sliced or chopped fresh strawberries

2 tablespoons dry-roasted sunflower kernels

HOW TO MAKE IT

1 Use your fingers to carefully split each pita half open (but do not break into 2 pieces) to form a pocket.

2 Use the knife to spread peanut butter inside the pita pockets. Use the spoon to divide the raisins, strawberries, and sunflower kernels among the pockets. Serve the pockets immediately or wrap with plastic wrap and chill up to 6 hours.

Makes 4 servings

This protein-packed pouch will keep you running through all of your afternoon and evening activities.

THAT'S A WRAP

UTENSILS

Cutting board
Measuring cups
Measuring spoons
Table knife
Sharp knife
Plastic wrap, if you like

INGREDIENTS

4 7- to 8-inch flour tortillas
½ cup peanut butter
1 cup chopped red and/or green apple
¼ cup low-fat granola

PB AND A WRAP

HOW TO MAKE IT

1 Place the tortillas on the cutting board (you may need to do this in two batches). Use the table knife to spread 2 tablespoons of the peanut butter over each tortilla.

2 Sprinkle each tortilla with ¼ cup of the apple and 1 tablespoon of the granola.

3 Roll up the tortillas tightly. Cut each tortilla in half with the sharp knife. Serve wraps immediately or wrap the tortillas tightly in the plastic wrap and chill up to 24 hours.

Makes 4 servings

NUTRITION FACTS PER SERVING:
254 calories, 14 g total fat, 0 mg cholesterol,
234 mg sodium, 28 g carbohydrate, 3 g fiber, 8 g protein

UTENSILS

Cutting board
Table knife
Measuring cups
Measuring spoons
Plastic wrap

INGREDIENTS

12   thin slices cooked turkey

½   cup flavored reduced-fat cream cheese (½ of an 8-ounce tub)

1   medium carrot, cut into thin lengthwise strips

4   thin, lengthwise pickle slices

4   soft breadsticks (6 to 8 inches long)

   Leaf lettuce, if you like

HOW TO MAKE IT

1 On the cutting board overlap 3 turkey slices so meat is the same length as a breadstick. Use the knife to spread 2 tablespoons of the cream cheese on the turkey.

2 Place 1 carrot strip, 1 pickle slice, and 1 breadstick on the edge of the turkey. Roll up so the meat is wrapped around the breadstick. If you like, roll 1 or 2 lettuce leaves around the outside of the wrap. Repeat with the remaining ingredients to make 4 wraps. Wrap each sandwich tightly in the plastic wrap and chill 30 minutes to 24 hours.

Makes 4 servings

When you're hit by a serious snack attack, wrap it up with one of these twisted tempters.

NUTRITION FACTS PER SERVING:
228 calories, 6 g total fat, 26 mg cholesterol, 856 mg sodium, 28 g carbohydrate, 1 g fiber, 14 g protein

FRUIT AND CHEESE PITAS

UTENSILS

Cutting board
Sharp knife
Measuring cups
Small mixing bowl
Wooden spoon
Small spoon

INGREDIENTS

2   small kiwifruits or
    ½ cup strawberries

½   cup low-fat cottage cheese

¼   cup shredded reduced-fat
    cheddar cheese

¼   cup drained pineapple tidbits

1   large pita bread round,
    halved crosswise

2   tablespoons toasted sliced
    almonds, pecan pieces, or
    walnut pieces, if you like

A stuffed pita pocket makes the perfect one-handed hunger stopper.

HOW TO MAKE IT

1   If you are using the kiwi, have an adult remove the peel. Place the kiwi on the cutting board. Use the sharp knife to cut into small pieces. If you are using the strawberries, place them on the cutting board. Use the sharp knife to cut off the green tops. Throw the green tops away. Cut the strawberries into small pieces.

2   Put kiwi or strawberry pieces, cottage cheese, cheddar cheese, and pineapple tidbits into the bowl. Use the wooden spoon to combine.

3   Use your fingers to carefully split each pita half open (but do not break into 2 pieces) to form a pocket. Use the small spoon to scoop the fruit and cheese mixture into the pita pockets. If you like, sprinkle with almonds, pecans, or walnuts. Serve the pitas immediately.

Makes 2 servings

NUTRITION FACTS PER SERVING:
250 calories, 6 g total fat, 17 mg cholesterol, 482 mg sodium, 34 g carbohydrate, 4 g fiber, 14 g protein

CINNAMON BAGEL STICKS

Stick it to hunger with these simple and speedy bagel snacks. Dunk them in strawberry jam, if you like.

NUTRITION FACTS PER SERVING:
198 calories, 6 g total fat, 15 mg cholesterol, 279 mg sodium, 30 g carbohydrate, 1 g fiber, 5 g protein

UTENSILS

Toaster
Cutting board
Serrated knife
Large resealable plastic bag
Measuring spoons

INGREDIENTS

1   4-inch plain,
    cinnamon-raisin, egg, or
    poppy seed bagel,
    split in half

1   tablespoon butter or
    margarine, melted

1   tablespoon granulated sugar

½   teaspoon ground cinnamon

HOW TO MAKE IT

1   Toast the bagel halves in the toaster; let them cool a little. Place the bagel halves on the cutting board. Use the serrated knife to slice the bagel halves into ¼- to ½-inch-wide strips.

2   Put the bagel strips in the resealable plastic bag. Drizzle with melted butter or margarine. Seal the bag and shake to coat. Open the bag and sprinkle the sugar and cinnamon over the bagel strips. Reseal the bag and shake to coat again. Serve the bagel sticks immediately.

Makes 2 servings

TWISTED BREADSTICKS

NUTRITION FACTS PER SERVING:
95 calories, 3 g total fat, 5 mg cholesterol,
199 mg sodium, 15 g carbohydrate,
0 g fiber, 2 g protein

UTENSILS

Large baking sheet
Measuring spoons
Small mixing bowl
Small spoon
Pastry brush
Hot pads
Wire cooling rack
Pancake turner

INGREDIENTS

Nonstick cooking spray

2 tablespoons sugar

¼ teaspoon ground cinnamon

1 11-ounce package
refrigerated soft breadsticks
(12 breadsticks)

2 tablespoons butter or
margarine, melted

Applesauce or fruit preserves,
if you like

HOW TO MAKE IT

1 Turn on the oven to 375°F. Coat the baking sheet with nonstick cooking spray. Save until Step 3.

2 Put the sugar and cinnamon in the bowl. Use the spoon to combine. Brush each breadstick with the melted butter or margarine using the pastry brush. Sprinkle each breadstick with the sugar mixture. With your fingers, twist each breadstick several times.

3 Place the breadsticks on the baking sheet. Place the baking sheet in the oven. Bake for 10 to 13 minutes or until golden brown. Turn off the oven. Use the hot pads to remove the baking sheet from the oven. Place the baking sheet on the cooling rack. Use the pancake turner to remove the breadsticks from the baking sheet. If you like, serve with applesauce or preserves.

Makes 12 twists

Parmesan Twists:

Prepare as above except omit sugar, cinnamon, and applesauce or preserves. Sprinkle breadsticks with 2 to 3 tablespoons grated Parmesan cheese after brushing with butter. Twist and bake as above. Serve with warmed pizza sauce or cheese dip for dipping.

When you're looking for a snack that's totally twisted, choose your flavor combo and give these breadsticks a try.

HAVE A BALL

UTENSILS

Measuring cups
Measuring spoons
Shallow dish
Small spoon
Cutting board
Table knife
Large baking sheet
Hot pads
Pancake turner
Serving platter

INGREDIENTS

¼ cup granulated sugar or yellow- and/or orange-color sugar

½ teaspoon pumpkin pie spice

1 11½-ounce package refrigerated soft breadsticks (8 breadsticks)

48 mini chocolate chips

NUTRITION FACTS PER SERVING:
119 calories, 3 g total fat, 0 mg cholesterol,
193 mg sodium, 21 g carbohydrate,
0 g fiber, 2 g protein

SHRUNKEN PUMPKINS

HOW TO MAKE IT

1 Turn on the oven to 350°F. Put sugar and pumpkin pie spice in the shallow dish. Use the spoon to combine.

2 Unroll and separate the breadsticks. Put the breadsticks on the cutting board. Use the knife to cut each breadstick into 1-inch pieces. Roll each piece in the sugar mixture to coat the pieces on all sides. Place on the ungreased baking sheet.

3 Place the baking sheet in the oven. Bake about 10 minutes or until the bottoms are light brown. Turn off the oven. Use the hot pads to remove the baking sheet from the oven. Use the pancake turner to move the pumpkins to the serving platter. While still warm, top each pumpkin with one chocolate chip. Serve the pumpkins warm.

Makes 12 servings (48 pieces)

UTENSILS

Measuring cups

Measuring spoons

Small mixing bowl

Small spoon

Large baking sheet

Hot pads

Pancake turner

INGREDIENTS

2	10- to 12-ounce package refrigerated biscuits (20 total)
40	milk chocolate kisses
2/3 to 3/4	cup miniature marshmallows
1/4	cup sugar
2	teaspoons ground cinnamon

NUTRITION FACTS PER SERVING:
177 calories, 8 g total fat, 3 mg cholesterol,
316 mg sodium, 23 g carbohydrate,
1 g fiber, 3 g protein

CHOCOLATE SHOCK BISCUITS

HOW TO MAKE IT

1 Turn on the oven to 350°F. Use the palm of your hand to flatten the biscuits. Place 2 chocolate kisses and 3 or 4 marshmallows in the center of each biscuit. Use your fingers to bring the edges of the biscuit up and around the chocolate kisses and marshmallows to enclose; pinch the dough well to seal it shut.

2 Put the sugar and cinnamon in the bowl. Use the spoon to combine. Roll each biscuit in the sugar mixture to coat. Place biscuits on the ungreased baking sheet.

3 Place the baking sheet in the oven. Bake about 15 minutes or until the bottoms are golden brown. Turn off the oven. Use the hot pads to remove the baking sheet from the oven. Use the pancake turner to remove the biscuits from the baking sheet. Serve the biscuits warm.

Makes 20 biscuits

You don't have to juggle a lot of ingredients to impress everyone with these cool dough ball creations.

CHERRY CHOCOLATE CHIP COOKIES

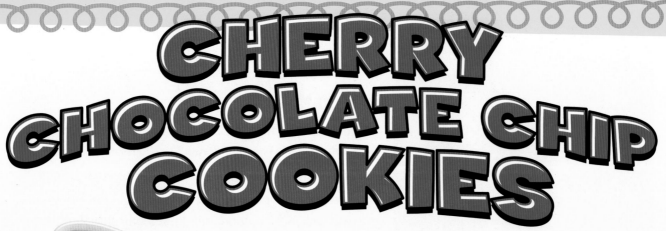

When you add chunks of cherry, this classic cookie gets some kicked-up flavor!

UTENSILS

Large mixing bowl
Electric mixer
Measuring cups
Measuring spoons
Rubber scraper
Wooden spoon
Cookie sheets
Hot pads
Pancake turner
Wire cooling rack

INGREDIENTS

½   cup butter or margarine, softened
½   cup granulated sugar
½   cup packed brown sugar
½   teaspoon baking soda
½   teaspoon salt
1   egg
1   teaspoon vanilla
1½   cups all-purpose flour
½   12-ounce package semisweet chocolate pieces
½   cup dried cherries

HOW TO MAKE IT

1   Turn on the oven to 375°F. Put butter in the bowl. Beat butter or margarine with the electric mixer on medium speed about 30 seconds or until the butter is softened. Turn off the mixer. Add granulated sugar, brown sugar, baking soda, and salt to the bowl. Beat on medium speed until combined. Turn off the mixer now and then and use the rubber scraper to scrape the sides of bowl. Turn off the mixer.

2   Add the egg and vanilla to the bowl. Beat on medium speed until combined. Turn off the mixer. Start adding flour, beating in as much of the flour as you can with the mixer. Turn off the mixer. Stir in any remaining flour with the wooden spoon. Stir in chocolate pieces and cherries.

3   Drop the dough by rounded teaspoons 2 inches apart on the ungreased cookie sheet. Put the cookie sheet in the oven and bake for 9 minutes or until the edges are golden. Use the hot pads to remove the cookie sheet from the oven. Cool the cookies on the cookie sheet for 1 minute. Use the pancake turner to move the cookies to the wire rack. Repeat with remaining dough. If using just 1 cookie sheet, let it cool between batches. Turn off the oven.

Makes 24 cookies

NUTRITION FACTS PER SERVING:
136 calories, 6 g total fat, 19 mg cholesterol, 206 mg sodium, 20 g carbohydrate, 1 g fiber, 2 g protein

ALL-AMERICAN APPLE PIE BARS

UTENSILS

Cutting board
Sharp knife
8x8x2-inch baking pan
Can opener
Measuring spoons
Medium bowl
Wooden spoon
Fork
Pastry brush
Hot pads
Wire cooling rack
Measuring cups
Small bowl
Wire whisk

INGREDIENTS

1   15-ounce package rolled
    refrigerated piecrusts
    (2 crusts)

1   21-ounce can apple pie filling

½   teaspoon ground cinnamon

    Fat-free milk

½   cup powdered sugar

1   tablespoon fat-free milk

NUTRITION FACTS PER SERVING:
171 calories, 7 g total fat, 3 mg cholesterol, 126 mg sodium,
26 g carbohydrate, 0 g fiber, 1 g protein

HOW TO MAKE IT

1 Turn on the oven to 375°F. Take piecrusts out of the package and place on the cutting board. Allow piecrusts to stand at room temperature for 15 minutes. Unroll piecrusts. Use the knife to trim the rounded edges of the piecrusts to make 9-inch squares. Throw away the scraps.

2 Put 1 piecrust in the baking pan. Use your fingers to press the piecrust into the sides of the pan. Put the pie filling and cinnamon in the medium bowl. Use the wooden spoon to combine. Spoon apple mixture into the piecrust-lined pan. Top with remaining piecrust. Fold the edges under and press into the piecrust on the sides of the pan. Prick the top piecrust all over with the fork. Use the pastry brush to brush lightly with the milk.

3 Place the pan in the oven. Bake for 45 minutes or until the crust is golden. Turn off the oven. Use the hot pads to remove the pan from the oven. Place the pan on the wire rack.

4 Put the powdered sugar and the 1 tablespoon milk in the small bowl. Use the whisk to combine to make a thin glaze. Use the pastry brush to brush glaze over the warm bars. Cool completely on the wire rack. Use the knife to cut into bars.

Makes 16 bars

From sea to shining sea, apple pie is an American classic. With all the flavor of a pie, these bars are a surefire favorite!

FRUIT FROM THE TROPICS SALAD

These sweet, juicy fruits give you a taste of tropical paradise.

UTENSILS

Can opener
Measuring cups
Medium bowl
Wooden spoon
Rubber scraper
Foil or plastic wrap
Measuring spoons, if you like

INGREDIENTS

1 8-ounce can pineapple chunks (juice pack), drained
½ cup miniature marshmallows
½ cup light dairy sour cream
1 11-ounce can mandarin orange sections, drained
1 tablespoon toasted shredded coconut, if you like

NUTRITION FACTS PER SERVING:
138 calories, 3 g total fat, 10 mg cholesterol, 33 mg sodium, 26 g carbohydrate, 1 g fiber, 3 g protein

HOW TO MAKE IT

1 Put the pineapple chunks, marshmallows, and sour cream in the bowl. Use the wooden spoon to combine. Use the rubber scraper to gently fold in the mandarin oranges.

2 Cover the bowl with foil or plastic wrap and chill 2 to 24 hours. If you like, before serving sprinkle with coconut.
Makes 4 side-dish servings

FRUIT-FILLED CHINESE WONTONS

NUTRITION FACTS PER SERVING:
44 calories, 1 g total fat, 1 mg cholesterol, 47 mg sodium,
9 g carbohydrate, 1 g fiber, 1 g protein

UTENSILS

Muffin pan with 24 1¾-inch muffin cups

Measuring spoons

Hot pads

Wire cooling rack

Measuring cups

Small saucepan

Rubber scraper

Small spoon

INGREDIENTS

Nonstick cooking spray

24 wonton wrappers

2 teaspoons sugar

¼ cup seedless raspberry preserves

¼ teaspoon ground cinnamon

1 cup fresh raspberries

⅔ cup small fresh blueberries

¼ cup packaged sliced almonds, if you like

HOW TO MAKE IT

1 Turn on the oven to 375°F. Lightly coat twenty-four 1¾-inch muffin cups with nonstick cooking spray. Press 1 wonton wrapper into each cup. Spray wonton wrappers with additional cooking spray and sprinkle with sugar.

2 Place the pan in the oven. Bake for 8 to 10 minutes or until crisp. Turn off the oven. Use the hot pads to remove the pan from the oven. Place the pan on the wire rack to cool wontons slightly. Remove the wontons from the cups. Cool completely on the wire rack.

3 Put preserves in the saucepan. Place the pan on the burner. Turn the burner to medium heat. Heat just until melted. Turn off the burner. Use the hot pads to remove the pan from the burner.

4 Use the rubber scraper to stir cinnamon into the melted preserves. Gently stir in raspberries and blueberries. Use the small spoon to divide the mixture evenly among the prepared wontons. Serve within 4 hours of filling. If you like, sprinkle each wonton with almonds just before serving.

Makes 24 servings

Next stop, China, where wonton wrappers are used for all sorts of treats. Here they make perfect berry pouches.

SAIL-THE-SEVEN-SEAS PASTA SALAD

Ahoy, matey! Sailors and landlubbers alike will scarf down this seaworthy salad.

NUTRITION FACTS PER SERVING:
219 calories, 8 g total fat, 10 mg cholesterol, 483 mg sodium, 29 g carbohydrate, 2 g fiber, 8 g protein

UTENSILS

Measuring cups

Medium saucepan

Hot pads

Colander

Medium mixing bowl

Wooden spoon

Foil or plastic wrap

Cutting board

Sharp knife

Small star-shape cookie cutter

INGREDIENTS

6   ounces medium macaroni shells (2 cups)

1   cup thinly sliced carrots

1   medium cucumber, shredded (remove seeds, if you like)

1   medium yellow sweet pepper, cut in small triangles or coarsely chopped

$1/3$ to $1/2$ cup bottled Italian salad dressing

4   ounces packaged processed cheese spread or American cheese

HOW TO MAKE IT

1   Cook macaroni in the saucepan according to the package directions. (To test the macaroni for doneness, remove one piece, let it cool slightly, and bite into it. The center will be soft, not chewy.) When macaroni is cooked, turn off the burner. Use the hot pads to remove the pan from the burner.

2   Place the colander in the sink. Pour macaroni into the colander to drain water. Rinse the drained macaroni with cold water; drain again.

3   Put cooked macaroni, carrots, cucumber, and sweet pepper in the bowl. Drizzle with Italian dressing. Use the wooden spoon to combine. Cover the bowl with foil or plastic wrap and chill 1 to 4 hours.

4   Place the cheese on the cutting board. Use the knife to cut cheese into $1/2$-inch slices. Use a small star-shape cookie cutter to cut cheese slices into small stars. Or use the knife to cut cheese slices into cubes. Toss cheese into the salad just before serving.

Makes 6 servings

MEXICAN QUESADILLAS

When you need a snacking fiesta, take a trip to Mexico with these filled tortillas.

NUTRITION FACTS PER SERVING:
148 calories, 5 g total fat, 15 mg cholesterol, 300 mg sodium,
14 g carbohydrate, 1 g fiber, 8 g protein

UTENSILS

Can opener
Measuring cups
Measuring spoons
Table knife
Medium skillet
Pancake turner
Cutting board
Hot pads
Sharp knife

INGREDIENTS

¼ cup canned fat-free refried beans

4 6- to 8-inch flour tortillas

¾ cup shredded reduced-fat sharp cheddar cheese (3 ounces)

Salsa, if you like

Sour cream, if you like

HOW TO MAKE IT

1 Use the table knife to spread 1 tablespoon of refried beans on half of a tortilla. Put tortilla, bean side up, in the skillet. Sprinkle with a fourth of the cheese. Place the skillet on the burner. Turn the burner to medium heat.

2 Cook tortilla about 3 minutes or until cheese begins to melt. Use the pancake turner to fold the tortilla in half and then flip the tortilla over. Cook 1 to 2 minutes more or until golden brown. Use the pancake turner to move the tortilla to the cutting board. Repeat with the remaining refried beans, tortillas, and cheese. Turn off the burner. Use the hot pads to remove the skillet from the burner.

3 Use the sharp knife to cut each quesadilla into 3 wedges. Use the pancake turner to remove the quesadilla wedges from the skillet. If you like, serve with salsa and/or sour cream.

Makes 4 servings

AUSSIE SAUCY MEATBALLS

NUTRITION FACTS PER SERVING:
210 calories, 15 g total fat,
44 mg cholesterol, 759 mg sodium,
10 g carbohydrate, 2 g fiber, 9 g protein

UTENSILS

Can opener
Measuring spoons
Large saucepan with lid
Wooden spoon
Hot pads

INGREDIENTS

1   15-ounce can tomato sauce
2   tablespoons packed
    brown sugar
1   tablespoon yellow mustard
1   teaspoon chili powder
¼   teaspoon garlic salt
    Dash ground black pepper
1   16-ounce package frozen
    cooked meatballs

HOW TO MAKE IT

1   Put the tomato sauce, brown sugar, mustard, chili powder, garlic salt, and pepper in the saucepan. Use the wooden spoon to combine. Stir in the meatballs.

2   Place the saucepan on the burner. Turn the burner to medium heat. Cook until boiling. Turn the burner to low heat and cover the pan with the lid. Simmer for 15 minutes or until meatballs are heated through. Turn off the burner. Use the hot pads to remove the pan from the burner.

Makes 8 to 10 servings

This snacking adventure takes you Down Under to the Australian outback. Share the meaty snack with your best mates.

73

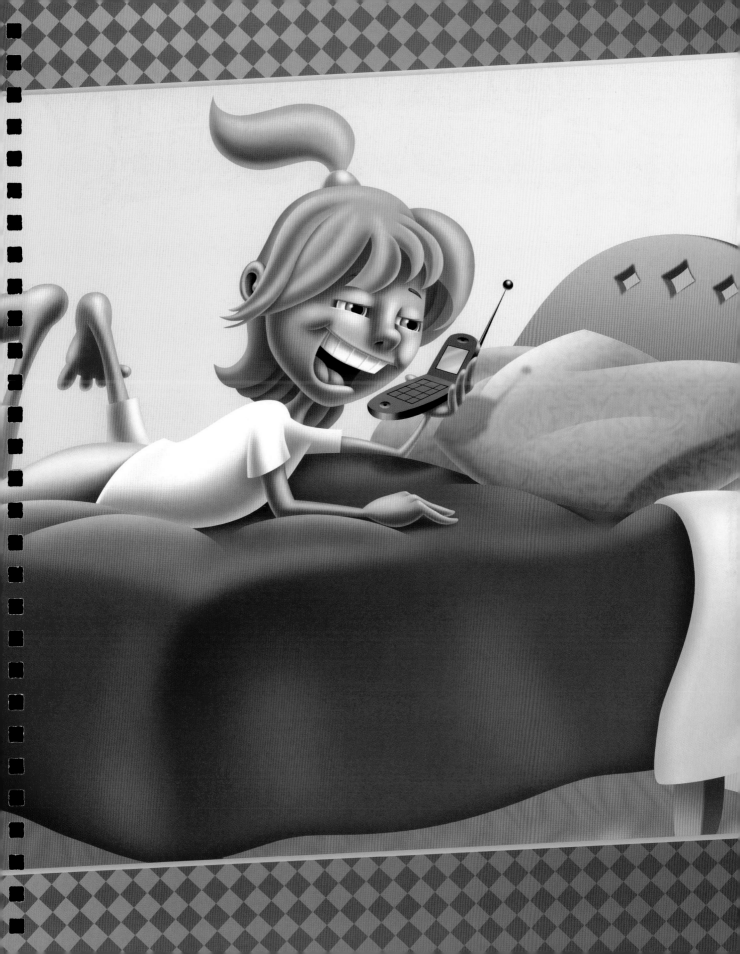

CHOCONUTTY SANDWICHES

NUTRITION FACTS PER SERVING:
120 calories, 6 g total fat, 0 mg cholesterol,
82 mg sodium, 14 g carbohydrate,
1 g fiber, 3 g protein

UTENSILS

Measuring cups
Measuring spoons
Small mixing bowl
Wooden spoon
Table knife
Airtight storage container

INGREDIENTS

½   cup chunky peanut butter
¼   cup plain low-fat yogurt
¼   cup chocolate syrup
½   teaspoon vanilla
32 vanilla wafers

HOW TO MAKE IT

1   Put peanut butter, yogurt, chocolate syrup, and vanilla in the bowl. Use the wooden spoon to combine. Use the knife to spread the peanut butter mixture on the flat side of half the vanilla wafers. Top with the remaining vanilla wafers, flat side down. Store any leftover peanut butter mixture in the airtight container in the refrigerator up to 3 days.

Makes 16 sandwich cookies

Invite your best friends and go nuts with these chocolatey peanut butter bites!

NUTS-ABOUT-FRUIT SALAD

Next time you have friends over, mix things up with this totally sweet fruit toss.

NUTRITION FACTS PER SERVING:
135 calories, 6 g total fat, 1 mg cholesterol, 43 mg sodium, 19 g carbohydrate, 3 g fiber, 4 g protein

HOW TO MAKE IT

1   Put the large bowl in the sink. Place the colander over the large bowl. Put pineapple with juice in colander and drain juice into the bowl. Use the measuring spoons to save 1 tablespoon of the pineapple juice. Save drained pineapple until Step 2 and save juice until Step 3.

2   Put drained pineapple, carrot, apple or pear, sunflower seeds, and raisins or cherries in the medium bowl. Use the wooden spoon to combine.

3   Put yogurt and peanut butter in the small bowl. Use the wooden spoon to combine. Stir in the reserved pineapple juice. Pour the yogurt mixture over the pineapple mixture; stir gently to combine. Place in the airtight container and chill 1 to 4 hours.

Makes 6 servings

MINI FRUITY TARTS

Stuffed with your favorite fruits, these bite-size sweets make perfect party treats!

UTENSILS

Cutting board
Sharp knife
Small bowl
Measuring cups
Wooden spoon
Small spoon
Measuring spoons

INGREDIENTS

1 large banana, 2 kiwifruit, and/or 1 cup strawberries

1 8-ounce tub cream cheese

¼ cup strawberry, peach, pineapple, or other preserves

1 2.1-ounce package miniature phyllo dough shells (15 shells)

3 tablespoons chocolate ice cream topping

NUTRITION FACTS PER SERVING:
86 calories, 3 g total fat, 7 mg cholesterol, 86 mg sodium, 11 g carbohydrate, 0 g fiber, 2 g protein

HOW TO MAKE IT

1 If you are using the banana, remove the peel and throw away. Place the banana on the cutting board. Use the knife to cut the banana into small pieces. If you are using the kiwi, have an adult remove the peel. Place the kiwi on the cutting board. Use the knife to cut into small pieces. If you are using the strawberries, place them on the cutting board. Use the knife to cut off the green tops. Throw the green tops away. Cut the strawberries into small pieces.

2 Put cream cheese and preserves in the small bowl. Use the wooden spoon to combine. Use the small spoon to spoon some of the cream cheese mixture into each phyllo shell.

3 Divide the fruit among the shells. Drizzle some of the ice cream topping over fruit.

Makes 15 tarts

FRUIT-CICLES

NUTRITION FACTS PER SERVING:
50 calories, 0 g total fat, 0 mg cholesterol, 4 mg sodium,
12 g carbohydrate, 1 g fiber, 0 g protein

UTENSILS

Measuring cups

Measuring spoons

Electric blender

8 3-ounce paper or plastic drink cups or pop molds

8x8x2- or 9x9x2-inch baking pan (if using drink cups)

Foil

Sharp knife

Wooden sticks

INGREDIENTS

2½   cups cubed, seeded watermelon, cantaloupe, or honeydew melon

¼   cup fresh or frozen raspberries, thawed

¼   cup sugar

1   tablespoon lemon juice

Fresh or frozen raspberries, thawed, if you like

HOW TO MAKE IT

1   Put melon, raspberries, sugar, and lemon juice in the blender. Cover the blender with the lid and blend on high speed until smooth. Turn off the blender. If you like, place 3 to 5 raspberries into each cup or pop mold. Pour the blended fruit mixture into the cups or molds.

2   If using the cups, place the cups on the baking pan. Cover each cup or mold with foil. Use the knife to make a small hole in the center of the foil. Slide a wooden stick through the hole into the fruit mixture in each cup.

3   Place the baking pan or pop molds in the freezer. Freeze for at least 6 hours or overnight until the pops are firm. Remove from the freezer. Remove the foil and tear paper cups away or remove the pops from the molds.

Makes 8 servings

Need to chill out? Lick hunger with these frozen fruity pops.

PARTY MIX-UPS

UTENSILS

Measuring cups
Large bowl
Wooden spoon
Airtight storage container

INGREDIENTS

1½ cups cinnamon-flavor bear-shape graham snack cookies

½ cup raisins

½ cup dried tart cherries

½ cup candy-coated milk chocolate pieces or semisweet chocolate pieces

¼ cup chopped dried pineapple

NUTRITION FACTS PER SERVING:
351 calories, 8 g total fat, 2 mg cholesterol,
125 mg sodium, 68 g carbohydrate,
3 g fiber, 3 g protein

BEAR-Y SWEET SNACK

HOW TO MAKE IT

1 Put graham snack cookies, raisins, cherries, chocolate pieces, and pineapple in the bowl. Use the wooden spoon to combine.

2 Spoon the cookie mixture into the airtight container. Store at room temperature up to 24 hours or in the refrigerator up to 2 days.

Makes 3¼ cups

Call your friends and invite them over to share these crunchy concoctions.

NUTRITION FACTS PER SERVING:
80 calories, 6 g total fat, 5 mg cholesterol,
165 mg sodium, 5 g carbohydrate,
1 g fiber, 2 g protein

CRUNCHY MUNCH MIX

HOW TO MAKE IT

1 Turn on the oven to 300°F. Put cheese crackers and wheat crackers in the roasting pan. Place the pan in the oven. Bake about 5 minutes or until warm. Use the hot pads to remove the pan from the oven.

2 Add pretzel twists and nuts to the pan. Pour melted butter or margarine over the mixture and sprinkle with salad dressing mix. Use the wooden spoon to combine. Use the hot pads to place the pan back in the oven. Bake for 10 minutes more. Use the hot pads to remove the pan from the oven. Use the wooden spoon to stir the mixture. Use the hot pads to return the pan to the oven. Bake for 10 minutes more. Turn off the oven. Use the hot pads to remove the pan from the oven.

3 Pour the mixture on the foil to cool. Store in the airtight container at room temperature up to 1 week.

Makes 13 cups

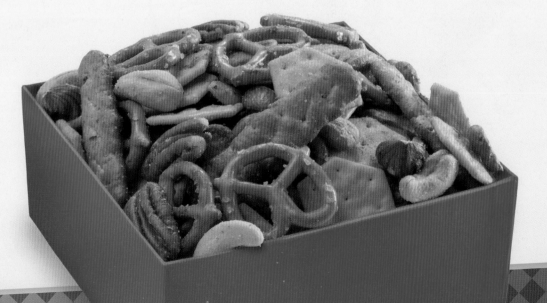

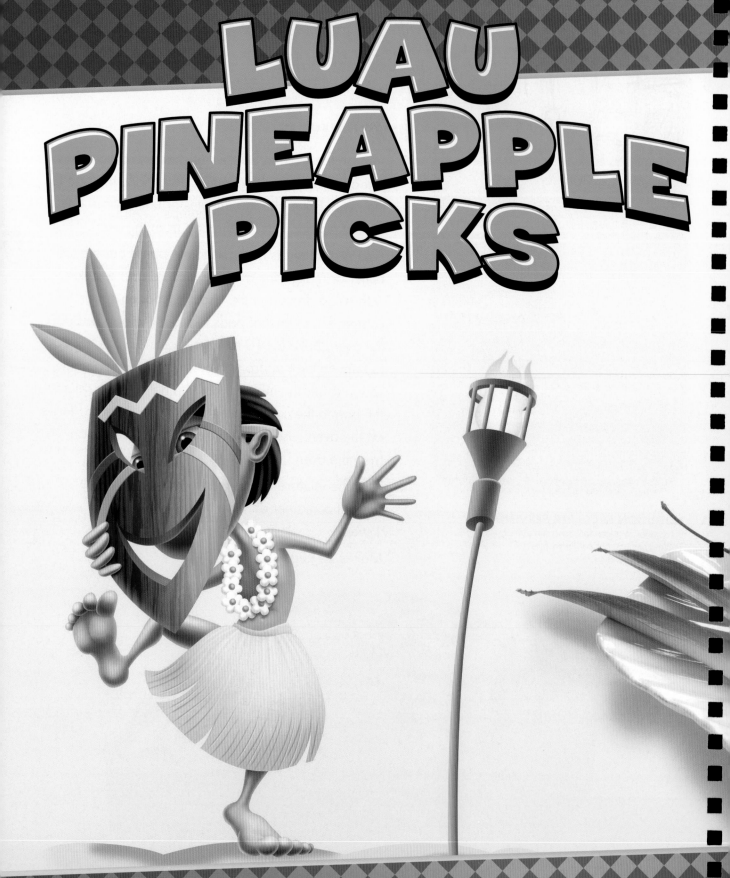

LUAU PINEAPPLE PICKS

UTENSILS

Can opener

Measuring cups

Medium bowl

Wooden spoon

Wooden toothpicks

Foil or plastic wrap, if you like

INGREDIENTS

1   15 ¼-ounce can pineapple chunks (juice pack), drained

¼   cup orange marmalade

6   ounces thinly sliced cooked ham, cut into 4x1½-inch strips

1   10-ounce jar maraschino cherries, drained

HOW TO MAKE IT

1   Put pineapple chunks and orange marmalade in the bowl. Use the wooden spoon to combine.

2   Wrap a ham strip around each pineapple chunk. Thread each chunk onto a toothpick. Add a maraschino cherry to each toothpick. Serve immediately or cover with the foil or plastic wrap and chill up to 2 hours.

Makes about 36 servings

NUTRITION FACTS PER SERVING:
33 calories, 0 g total fat, 3 mg cholesterol, 63 mg sodium, 7 g carbohydrate, 0 g fiber, 1 g protein

Throw on a grass skirt and get ready to hula down with these festive kabobs that are perfect for a Hawaiian luau.

WINTER MINTY COCOA

NUTRITION FACTS PER SERVING:
118 calories, 2 g total fat, 1 mg cholesterol, 88 mg sodium,
24 g carbohydrate, 0 g fiber, 1 g protein

UTENSILS

Measuring cups

Medium saucepan

Wire whisk

Hot pads

Mugs

INGREDIENTS

8 cups water

1½ cups instant cocoa mix

½ cup butter mints, crushed

Whipped cream, if you like

Unsweetened cocoa powder, if you like

Peppermint sticks or candy canes, if you like

HOW TO MAKE IT

1 Pour water into the saucepan. Place the saucepan on the burner. Turn the burner to medium-high. Heat until the water just begins to boil. Use the whisk to stir in the cocoa mix and butter mints until mixture is well blended and mints are melted. Turn off the burner. Use hot pads to remove pan from burner.

2 Pour the cocoa into the mugs. Serve cocoa warm. If you like, top the cocoa with the whipped cream and cocoa powder. If you like, serve with peppermint sticks or candy canes.

Makes 8 to 10 servings

Stirring a warm mug of cocoa with a peppermint stick is the perfect way to celebrate a snowy day.

CUPCAKE NESTS

Hatch a great get-together with these edible nests for your guests to peck at!

NUTRITION FACTS PER SERVING:
267 calories, 12 g total fat, 1 mg cholesterol,
203 mg sodium, 37 g carbohydrate, 1 g fiber, 3 g protein

UTENSILS

Muffin pans with 12 2½-inch cups
Paper baking cups
Small spoon
Hot pads
Wire cooling rack
Table knife
Measuring cups

INGREDIENTS

1   package 2-layer-size cake mix with confetti sprinkles

1   16-ounce can chocolate or white frosting

1   cup candy-coated chocolate-covered peanuts

1½   cups toasted flaked or shredded coconut

HOW TO MAKE IT

1   Turn on the oven to 350°F. Line 24 2½-inch muffin cups with the paper baking cups. Save until Step 2.

2   Prepare the cake mix according to the directions on the package. Use the spoon to place the batter into the prepared muffin cups, filling each cup about one-half full. Bake the cupcakes according to the directions on the package. Turn off the oven. Use the hot pads to remove the pan from the oven. Cool cupcakes in the pan on the wire rack. Remove the cupcakes from the pan.

3   Use the knife to spread the tops of the cooled cupcakes with the frosting. Place the chocolate-covered peanuts in cupcake centers for eggs. Sprinkle the coconut on top of the cupcakes to resemble nests.

Makes 24 cupcakes

TOP-IT-OFF BROWNIES

UTENSILS

8x8x2-inch baking pan
Medium saucepan
Wooden spoons
Measuring cups
Hot pads
Measuring spoons
Small bowl
Rubber scraper
Wooden toothpicks
Wire cooling rack

INGREDIENTS

Shortening
½ cup butter
3 ounces unsweetened chocolate
1 cup sugar
2 eggs
1 teaspoon vanilla
⅔ cup all-purpose flour
¼ teaspoon baking soda
½ of a 15- to 16-ounce container frosting, if you like
Choice of brownie toppings (see right)

HOW TO MAKE IT

1 Turn on the oven to 350°F. Grease the baking pan with shortening. Save until Step 5.

2 Put butter and chocolate in the saucepan. Place the saucepan on the burner. Turn burner to low heat. Cook until melted. Stir frequently with the wooden spoon. Turn off the burner. Use the hot pads to remove the saucepan from the burner. Cool mixture to room temperature.

3 Use the wooden spoon to stir sugar into cooled chocolate mixture. Add eggs, 1 at a time, beating with the wooden spoon just until combined. Stir in vanilla.

4 Use a clean wooden spoon to combine the flour and baking soda in the bowl. Add flour mixture to chocolate mixture in saucepan. Stir until combined.

5 Spoon batter into prepared pan, spreading evenly with the wooden spoon. Use the rubber scraper to scrape all the batter out of the saucepan.

6 Put the pan in the oven. Bake about 30 minutes or until a wooden toothpick comes out clean. (To test doneness, use the hot pads to pull out oven rack. Stick the toothpick in the center of the brownies; pull out the toothpick. If any brownie sticks to it, bake brownies a few minutes more; test again.) Turn off oven. Use the hot pads to remove the baking pan from the oven. Place the pan on the wire rack to cool. Top brownies as you like.

Makes 16 brownies

Summer Banana Boat Brownies:

Use a table knife to spread half of a 15- to 16-ounce container vanilla frosting onto cooled brownies. Remove the peel from 2 small bananas. Throw away the peels. Place bananas on cutting board. Use a sharp knife to thinly slice bananas. Place 1 cup fresh strawberries on cutting board. Remove stems. Use the sharp knife to slice strawberries. Arrange bananas and strawberry slices in a decorative pattern on frosting. Sprinkle with 2 tablespoons peanuts. If you like, add a few maraschino cherries. Serve immediately or chill in the refrigerator up to 30 minutes.

Celebration Candy Bar Brownies:

Use a table knife to spread half of a 15- to 16-ounce container vanilla or chocolate frosting onto cooled brownies. On a cutting board use a sharp knife to cut candy bars into small pieces (you will need about 1 cup chopped candy bars). Choose chocolate-covered English toffee, chocolate-covered crisp wafers, candy-coated milk chocolate pieces, chocolate-covered peanut butter cups, malted milk balls, chocolate-coated caramel-topped nougat bars, and/or chocolate-covered nougat bars with peanuts. Sprinkle chopped candy bars over frosting.

Pretty-in-Pink Brownies:

Spoon half of a 15- to 16-ounce container vanilla frosting into a small mixing bowl. Stir in a few drops of red food coloring to tint the frosting pink. Use a table knife to spread pink frosting onto cooled brownies. Or frost cooled brownies with one 8-ounce tub strawberry cream cheese. Arrange ¼ cup tiny pink and/or white marshmallows on frosting. Sprinkle with 1 to 2 tablespoons pink nonpareils, pink-color sugar, and/or small pink decorative candies. If using cream cheese, chill brownies in refrigerator until ready to serve.

Here's a sweet treat sure to wow a crowd. Stock up on a bunch of toppings so guests can design their own desserts.

NUTRITION FACTS PER SERVING:
216 calories, 12 g total fat, 43 mg cholesterol,
115 mg sodium, 26 g carbohydrate, 1 g fiber, 2 g protein

93

INDEX

MY FAVORITE RECIPES LIST